Planning a Moon Garden

Marcella Shaffer

CONTENTS

Introduction

If you're like most of us, you work during the day. If you're also a gardener, that means you miss viewing and enjoying your garden during its prime time: the daylight hours. There is a way, however, to enjoy the full effect of your labor without quitting your job: Plant a night-blooming garden, otherwise known as a moon garden. Moon gardens are designed expressly for evening and nighttime enjoyment.

Although a moon garden is attractive at any time of day, at dusk it takes on a whole new look and feel, casting an almost magical spell. Alluring fragrances intermingle, enticing you to visit and discover their source. Comfortable seating invites relaxation, urging you to sit and admire the pale colors of the flowers and foliage as reflecting light from the setting sun and the rising moon gives the garden an almost mystical glow. Is it any wonder that Victorian green thumbs, who are generally credited with developing moon gardens, referred to them as "dream gardens"?

A night-blooming fragrant garden offers a peaceful and tranquil spot to rest and relax. It can be elaborate or simple, large or small. Even an out-of-the-way corner beside a garage or shed or a small section of lawn can be transformed into a moon garden. If you have limited gardening space, never fear: Many night-blooming plants grow well in containers, and your patio or deck can become a spectacular moon garden — your own private haven from the world.

A Garden of Unearthly Delights

The most important aspects of a moon garden are the joy and relaxation you derive from it. However, a garden can provide only the setting; the rest is up to you. Forget about the day's struggles and problems; let your mind unwind and all your senses soar. Inhale the flowers' perfumes. Watch with fascination as the plants become luminous with the fading of daylight and the arrival of moonlight. Touch the shimmering foliage. Hear the soft flutter of a moth's wings as it alights on a blossom or the soothing tinkling of a garden fountain. Taste a drop of dew with your tongue. A moon garden has endless pleasures to offer the mind and soul. If you wish to share your haven with others, this garden is the perfect place for a casual summer party or an evening reception — or a romantic tryst!

Designing Your Moon Garden

Designing a moon garden is not as difficult as it might seem. This type of garden isn't intended to be showy or to attract attention. Rather, it's intended for your own pleasure. There is no right or wrong way to create a moon garden, so cater to your personal tastes and enjoyment. An occasional short plant tucked in behind a taller one won't hurt at all, and if a particular plant doesn't please you, simply change it. If you're happy in the garden you've created and savor the time you spend in it, your moon garden is a success.

As with all gardens, a moon garden needs to be planned out in a logical sequence. First comes what is known to garden designers as the *hardscape* — the garden's physical shape plus any walls and other structures, water features, and paths. Then comes the *landscape* — the plants, ornaments, and seating.

The following design considerations are intended only as a guide to help you start creating your own moon garden. Remember, the most important consideration is that you enjoy the experience.

Location

The location of the garden is an extremely important factor. It's essential that the site gives you a place to relax yet is convenient enough to visit frequently. Look around your yard for a secluded spot or one that isn't visible to neighbors or the busy street. If you don't have such a place, create one — or the feeling of one. Use shrubs, fences, lattice panels, trellises, or other screening devices to create an illusion of privacy. You may also be able to use an existing structure, such as the side of your house or garage.

Pick a spot that makes the most of available natural lighting. Don't select a spot that receives less than six or seven hours of sunshine daily. Even though most plants can survive in partial shade, many of them won't grow well without plenty of light. If you have to use a partly shaded area, choose plants suitable for growing under low-light conditions, such as impatiens, hosta, and astilbe.

Stroll through your yard in the daytime, early evening, and nighttime. Take into consideration sunlight, moonlight, and shadows before making a decision on location. In summer, the moon is low in the sky in the south. Observe the moon's progress over several nights, noting where it shines the brightest and is the least obstructed in its arc across the sky. Plan your garden so that there are few obstructions to the southeast, south, and southwest, allowing summer moonlight to illuminate your garden.

Form and Shape

After you've selected a location, next consider what form your garden will be and what will work best for your particular location. The most common forms of gardens are:

Border gardens are designed so that one side is against a structure, such as a wall or fence. They are viewed primarily from the front, with the shortest plants displayed in the front and along the sides.

Island gardens are surrounded on all sides by lawn or other open space. They are viewed from all sides and are usually centrally located. Island beds have the tallest plants in the center, the shortest plants along the edges, and intermediate-height plants in between. Island gardens require more intermediate and short plants than do corner or border gardens. For a more natural effect, slightly offset the center of the island.

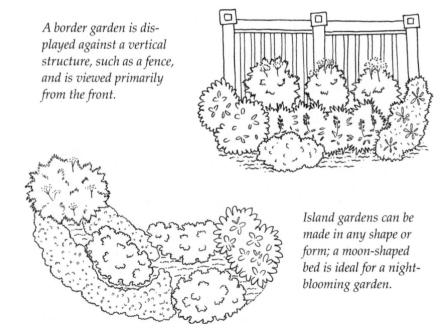

A border garden is displayed against a vertical structure, such as a fence, and is viewed primarily from the front.

Island gardens can be made in any shape or form; a moon-shaped bed is ideal for a night-blooming garden.

Corner gardens are designed to have two sides against a structure or formed by a structure, such as a fence or hedges. These gardens are viewed primarily from the front. Corner gardens can provide more privacy than island or border gardens, because you can actually sit inside them.

Moon gardens can be any size and follow any outline. They can be shaped asymmetrically to fit a corner or contour. Squared-off, symmetrical beds have a more formal appearance, while curving edges look more casual and natural. Before deciding which garden silhouette you prefer, lay out several different shapes.

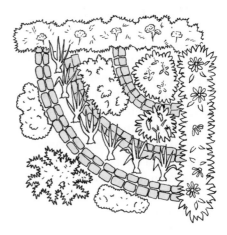

A corner garden that is meant to be viewed from the front can be terraced for maximum effect.

Use a garden hose to create the layout of an asymmetrical garden; use pegs and string to create a symmetrical plan. Remember that tight curves can make mowing and trimming more difficult; if you want to keep your yardwork simple, keep any curves in the garden border long and gentle.

Walk away and view the layout from different angles. When you've decided on the shape and size, sprinkle powdered lime, sand, or flour to mark the lines. Digging will be easier if the temporary markers aren't in the way.

Use smaller gardens to accent the layout of your larger garden. A white stepping-stone path leading to a bed of white roses edged with brick, for example, can be a dramatic focal point in a larger moon garden.

Water Features

Moonlight on water — whether it's a simple birdbath or a pond — is positively breathtaking. There is something about moonlight and water that naturally evokes a feeling of peace and relaxation. Even if you have limited space or plan to create a moon garden on your deck or patio, you can still have a water source.

Birdbaths. Birdbaths serve a dual purpose: They attract birds during the day and become a reflecting pool at night. A functional birdbath offers shallow water and a rough surface that allows birds to keep their footing. For the safety of your backyard birds, set the birdbath away from any shrubs or tall plants that could hide a stalking cat.

Garden ponds. Many garden-supply stores offer pond kits that you can install in a weekend. Available in a variety of shapes, sizes, and designs, these ponds can be incorporated into any moon garden. When space is limited, utilize a large pottery bowl or a half barrel lined with heavy-mil plastic.

If your garden isn't large enough for a full-size pond, use a half barrel to create a container water garden.

Fountains. The sound of a gurgling fountain or trickling waterfall is incredibly relaxing, and it can help drown out unwelcome neighborhood noises and the rumble of traffic. Flowing water also reflects light and creates movement, adding another visual attraction. In a more formal moon garden, a classic freestanding fountain that is prominently displayed or that sprays water from within a pool works beautifully. The type of nozzle you select determines the spray pattern.

A more casual moon garden can host an inconspicuous wall fountain or one made of rocks or other natural material. You can make your own by using a recirculating pump and vinyl tubing (available from garden-supply stores and many hardware stores). Use your imagination and creativity to make a fountain that suits your personal style and moon garden décor. Tabletop fountains are perfect for smaller gardens, because they are portable, attractive, and easy to install and maintain.

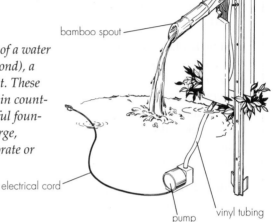

Fountains consist simply of a water reservoir (in this case, a pond), a pump, tubing, and a spout. These elements can be arranged in countless ways to create beautiful fountains, whether small or large, spouting or seeping, elaborate or simple.

bamboo spout

electrical cord

pump

vinyl tubing

Garden Paths

Paths and walkways invite you to enter a garden and see where they lead, creating a sense of destination. A linear path is best suited for a more structured or symmetrical moon garden. Curving and meandering paths are best suited for an informal or asymmetrical moon garden.

Use light-colored gravel or stepping-stones for paths in your moon garden, or plan for supplemental lighting. For a bit of whimsy, use stepping-stones in crescent moon and star shapes. Soften the path's edge with white rocks or low-growing plants.

To prevent weeds from sprouting in the pathway, lay a weed barrier, such as landscape fabric, underneath the flagstones or gravel. This will prevent weeds from emerging and keep the path from becoming muddy when it rains. Alternatively, plant aromatic groundcover herbs, such as thyme or Roman chamomile, in the cracks between the stones. Once these shrubby little plants have filled in, they'll require only occasional tidying up. As garden visitors pass down the path, they'll crush the herbs beneath their feet, releasing a wonderful fragrance.

Laying a Flagstone Path

Laying a flagstone path for your moon garden is a good weekend project. Choose square or rectangular stones for a formal garden or irregularly shaped stones for a more casual look. Whatever their style, the stones should be light or silvery in color, both to enhance the ghostly atmosphere of the moon garden and to help passersby find their footing in the darkness.

Step 1. Plan the path. Use a garden hose to test the path of your walkway. Keep the width of the path generally even for its duration. Sprinkle powdered limestone or sand on the ground to outline the path.

Step 2. Dig out the path. Remove the soil along the course of the path to a depth of at least 4 inches. If the path is going to be in an area that is particularly wet, you'll want to dig out a few more inches worth of soil to allow for extra drainage.

Step 1

Step 2

Step 3. Fill the base with drainage material. Shovel coarse stone or stone dust into the excavated area, tamping it firm as you go. Fill in with enough drainage material that the flagstones, when set in the path, will rise to just above ground level. Keep the level of drainage material as even as possible.

Step 3

Step 4

Step 4. Lay the stones. Lay the stones one by one on top of the drainage material, leaving about half an inch of space between stones. When you are pleased with the layout, tap each stone gently into place with a mallet.

Step 5. Fill in the cracks between the stones. Shovel coarse sand or stone dust on top of the flagstones. Sweep the sand or dust over the stones until the cracks between the stones are filled. Then mist the entire path with water. Repeat this process a few days later.

Step 5

Supplemental Lighting

Color results when light is reflected. Without light, even white flowers won't be visible after dark. This means that a lightless garden will be virtually featureless on moonless nights. For those evenings when there is no moonlight, or to add to the existing natural light, employ supplemental lighting.

A subtle source of lighting that imparts a diffused glow is usually the most effective and pleasing in a moon garden. Types of subtle light that work wonderfully are:

- Flickering lanterns
- Dim, soft bulbs
- A string of clear Christmas lights

You might also consider illuminating a particular object as a focal point of your garden. To get a preview of how this will look before you install the lighting, try shining a flashlight on the focal point. Statuary, trees, a trellis, or even prominent plants often look spectacular when highlighted.

Many types of lighting designed primarily for gardens are available. Most are low voltage and easily installed without the assistance of an electrician. You can also use nonelectric lighting, such as candles or oil lamps and lanterns, all of which provide subtle sources of light without the installation time and expense of electric lighting. Of course, when you're using flames as a source of light, be sure to suspend them in an appropriate holder away from grass, foliage, and other flammable objects, and never leave them burning unattended.

A low-wattage light set behind a garden ornament lends a soft glow, enhancing the mysterious and quiet atmosphere of a moon garden.

Garden Embellishments

Here's where your imagination can really go wild. Although a plants-only garden can certainly be attractive, adding other flourishes personalizes your garden and makes it even more appealing. These embellishments contribute to the garden's ambience and encourage you to visit more often and to stay longer.

Fences, Trellises, and Arbors

Besides providing support for plants, trellises can conceal problem areas, serve as accent pieces, or help define the garden's edges. Trellises can easily be attached to a wall, transforming a boring blank space into a beautiful home for a climbing vine covered with blooms. As a garden accent, a trellis can be fastened to sturdy legs in the ground and then positioned to serve as an archway into the garden or a seating area.

An arbor that serves as an entryway offers an invitation to visit the garden. As with other garden features, try to use white or light colors for your trellis or arbor.

An arbor with seating becomes a romantic evening hideaway.

Chimes

A lovely final addition to the moon garden is wind chimes. Hang them so that the slightest breeze will set off their melodic tones. The varieties and styles of chimes are almost endless, and each has its own individual sound. Select ones that appeal to your taste, both visually and aurally.

Ornaments and Statuary

Although garden ornaments and statuary aren't necessities in a moon garden, they can be wonderful additions. Accessorize your moon garden as you would your home — you are limited only by your imagination. White or light-colored ornaments work best, with marble or faux marble being exceptionally striking in the moonlight. If your garden style is more casual than formal, use whimsical pieces of statuary or playful folk art. Situate small pieces so that they can be appreciated close up.

A silvery gazing ball is at home in any garden, regardless of your decorating style or taste. Moonlight reflecting on this classic piece makes a dramatic impact while inviting quiet musings.

Seating

Benches and seats can be ornamental, but they must be comfortable and invite you to sit and enjoy the garden. Before deciding on your garden's seating, try out various benches and chairs. Many different styles are available, but unfortunately, not all of them are comfortable.

Use Light Colors on Furniture

Your garden furniture should reflect the dreamy, effervescent nature of the moon garden. To reflect this mood, and to make the furniture easier to find, paint your fences, chairs, and stools in light colors. Pastel pink and blue hues, whites, and warm cream colors are especially effective in night-blooming gardens.

How to Choose Plants
for a Night-Blooming Garden

In no garden is your choice of plants more important than in a moon garden. To make even the smallest or simplest garden an oasis of serenity, it needs a pleasing mixture of color, fragrance, and texture.

Color

Save fiery reds, dashing oranges, and bright yellows for dramatic impact elsewhere. The key to color in a moon garden is peace and relaxation. Whereas whites and pastels can seem faded or washed out in the sun's bright light, twilight and moonlight intensify these pale colors until they seem to glow. The delicate hues of the blossoms emerge while the darker stems and leaves recede, creating a slightly eerie but beautiful effect.

Using Foliage for Color

Plant color isn't limited to blossoms alone. Foliage plays an equally important role in the color of a moon garden. Moon gardeners often neglect to consider the impact that foliage can have. After dark, the pale silver leaves of dusty miller (*Artemisia stelleriana, Senecio cineraria*) appear to shimmer, and the green of variegated hosta leaves recede, leaving only their white borders visible.

Pale pinks and lavenders, soft blues, and cream-colored tones all seem subtly luminescent. The pastel hues of *Dianthus* 'Aqua' appear to shimmer when viewed in the twilight hours, and the creamy blossoms of the tropical calla lily (*Zantedeschia aethiopica*) seem suspended by the moonlight itself.

Fragrance

Fragrance in a moon garden should be as prominent as moonlight. In the intimate setting of a moon garden, fragrant plants persuade you to linger and delight in their scent. Some plants, such as moonflower, emit their fragrance only at night to attract pollinating moths — a bonus in a garden enjoyed in the day's waning hours. Other plants, such as garden phlox (*Phlox paniculata*) and stock (*Matthiola incana*), are aromatic both day and night.

Texture

While texture certainly relates to the look and feel of leaves and flowers, texture in a moon garden takes on special importance. The subdued light of the moon asks people to walk more cautiously, and this slowed pace, along with the overall dimness of color, encourages garden visitors to really see the textural appeal of a garden. The soft, fuzzy gray lamb's ears *(Stachys byzantina)* begs you to take the time to stroke its velvety leaves. The open and airy baby's breath (*Gypsophila* spp.) appears to be a floating mist in the moonlight. Graceful clumps of *Artemisia schmidtiana* 'Silvermound' dip and rustle with the slightest passing breeze. The alluring silvery aura and soft evening air combine with the texture of plants to create an arresting display.

Plant Layout

The most beautiful gardens are usually a combination of shrubs, annuals, and perennials. Intermixing perennials with annuals ensures a continuous display of color throughout the season, while shrubs provide architectural interest, often have beautiful blooms, and serve as darker backgrounds against which to display light-colored flowers of perennials and annuals.

Consider Height

Because the flowers will all seem various shades of pale in the moonlight, use height instead of color to add a sense of depth to your garden. Place tall plants to the rear of the bed and in front of large, dark elements. Place low-growing plants so that they accent the front of the flower bed and outline the paths and walkways with shades of white and silver.

If you want a dark background border of good height but don't have a fence or wall against which to situate your garden, consider erecting a trellis as a substitute, and cover it with a quick-growing annual vine, such as morning glory. In the dark of evening, the twining vines will form a shadowy palette against which white flowers will shine.

Pay close attention to the variety and species of the plants you choose for your moon garden, as height can differ radically between species in the same genus. As an example, *Artemisia ludoviciana* 'Silver King' reaches up to 3 feet in height, while *Artemisia schmidtiana* 'Silvermound' is only about 1 foot tall.

Place taller, darker plants in the rear of your garden and smaller plants in front to create a sense of depth. Low-lying, silver-foliaged plants are excellent for lining pathways.

How Many?

As a general rule, odd numbers of plants are visually more appealing to the eye. Try to plant in groups of three, five, seven, and so forth. An exception to this rule is a plant used as a specimen or a focal point. In this case, a single plant makes the most impact. For even more lush, abundant growth in a moon garden, space plants somewhat closer than normal.

Starting Your Garden

Now that you're finished with the planning, it's time to actually create the garden. Is the site ready for planting? If not, you'll need to prepare the new garden bed before you go out and buy plants or transplant them from other flower beds on your property. And if you are buying new plants, make sure that you know what to look for, and choose healthy, suitable ones.

Preparing the Garden Site

Begin by cutting through the sod with a spade along the bed's edges. Remove the sod and rototill or dig the area, removing rocks and other debris. You may consider doing an at-home or professional soil test at this time to evaluate the pH of your soil as well as the concentrations of essential nutrients. Once you know your soil's strengths and deficiencies, you can amend the soil properly, making it optimal for your garden plants.

The best garden soil is deeply dug, fertile, and well drained, with plenty of organic matter. Spreading rotted manure, compost, or leaf mold into the bed provides the organic matter needed to improve the soil's texture and viability and add nutrients. If other soil conditioners or fertilizers are desired, add them at this time. Rototill or dig the bed again to mix the soil and additives.

Tilling in organic matter helps create more fertile, well-drained soil.

Defining the Area

An edging strip around the growing bed defines it and keeps the grass out of the bed — and vice versa. This will save you hours of maintenance, leaving more time to enjoy the garden. The edging strip should be installed at or slightly above soil level. For more visual interest, consider using light-colored bricks or stones instead of commercial plastic edging. All are available at garden centers.

What to Look for When Buying Plants

When selecting plants, start with bedding plants for easier and quicker results. Usually, choosing one-year-old perennials ensures blooms the first year.

Healthy plants that have been given good care stand a better chance of surviving and thriving when planted in your garden. When selecting plants, examine the following, which signal a healthy — and an unhealthy — plant:

- **Number of buds.** An abundance of buds is a good sign for two reasons. First, it means that the plant will have lots of blooms. Second, if the plant is not yet in bloom, it will have time to establish a viable root system before directing its energy to blooming. This will ensure a long, healthy life.
- **Root systems.** Roots growing through the bottom of the container indicate that the plant has been in the container too long and may be overly stressed.
- **Foliage.** A plant's leaves should appear lush and fresh. Do not purchase plants that are drooping or that have wilted leaves. Do not purchase plants that have grown tall and spindly; such growth is an indication that the plant may be root bound or may have been grown in low light.
- **Signs of pests.** Holes or trails on the leaves, webs on the underside, scales on the leaves or stems, and powdery residue on the leaves are all signs of pests. Don't purchase plants that have infestation problems.

Planting

When planting a container-grown plant, submerge the container in water first and let it thoroughly moisten. Then place your hand over the top of the pot so that the stems and leaves are between your fingers. Turn the pot and plant upside down. The plant will slide out easily.

To remove a plant from its container, first moisten the soil, then gently slide the plant from the container, holding it at the stem just above the soil surface.

If you purchased plants in cell packs, water them well and then remove each plant by pushing up on the bottom of the cell. Remove only one plant at a time to prevent the roots from drying out while you're planting.

If possible, transplant on a cool or overcast day; a drizzly day is even better. This helps the transplant adjust to its new setting without stress from sun or heat. If you must transplant on a sunny day, do so late in the day.

The planting hole should be twice as wide as the plant's rootball one and a half times as deep. Place the plant in the hole and firm the soil around it. Water thoroughly.

Shovel a layer of mulch on top of the soil to retard weed growth, help retain moisture, and improve the garden's appearance.

A Moon Garden Plant Catalog

The following plants are all excellent choices for a moon garden because they bloom only at night, they have silver-toned foliage that becomes luminescent in the moonlight, or they have white or pale-colored flowers that stand out in the evening hours. This is not an exhaustive list by any means; however, the plants listed here are widely available and will grow in a range of climates and conditions. Check with your local gardening center for more suggestions of plants suitable for the particular vagaries of your specific location.

Seasonal Tip

As you think about which plants you'd like in your garden, take into account which plants bloom at which times. You'll want to plan either for all the blooms to coincide or for there to be continuous blooming throughout the growing season.

Plants with Silver-Hued Foliage

In a moon garden, foliage is as important as the flowers. Plants with silver-hued foliage are true standouts in a moon garden; their silvery tones pick up and reflect the light of the moon, creating a sense of shimmering movement wherever they are planted.

Artemisia (*Artemisia* spp.)
PLANT CYCLE: Perennial, Zones 3–8, depending on the species
PREFERENCES: Plant in full sun or partial shade; most artemisias will tolerate a wide range of soil conditions.

Artemisia is lovely in a moon garden because of the interesting texture of its silvery or white foliage. There are many species and varieties to choose from, each with different growth characteristics. *Artemisia schmidtiana* 'Silver-mound' grows in rounded mounds that can reach 12 inches high and spread 18 to 20 inches across. Its foliage is pale gray, light, and feathery. *A. absinthium* 'Lambrook Silver' has shiny silver foliage and reaches 30 inches in height. *A. lactiflora* grows to 5 feet tall and bears creamy flowers on graceful stems. *A. ludoviciana* 'Silver King' and 'Silver Queen' are a ghostly silvery gray in color and will reach up to 2 feet high; these are the artemisias prized for wreathmaking.

Dusty Miller (*Senecio cineraria*)
PLANT CYCLE: Perennial, Zones 8–10; grown as an annual elsewhere
PREFERENCES: Plant in full sun in fertile, well-drained soil.

There are many plants called dusty miller, but this tender perennial is the most common. Dusty miller grows in mounds that reach 12 to 24 inches tall. Its deeply cut, silvery gray, felted foliage is an eye-catcher in the moon garden. Some popular varieties include 'Alice', with silver-tinged leaves; 'Cirrus', with gray-green leaves; 'Silver Dust', with gray-white leaves; and 'Silver Queen', a compact variety with silver-white leaves.

Goatsbeard (*Aruncus dioicus*)
PLANT CYCLE: Perennial, Zones 3–8
PREFERENCES: Plant in partial shade in moist, rich soil.

Magnificent ivory-colored feathery plumes of flowers adorn this perennial, which blooms in early summer, reaching nearly 5 feet in height and spreading 18 to 24 inches. Goatsbeard particularly striking in the twilight. Some popular varieties include 'Kneiffii' and 'Zweiweltenkind'.

Hosta (*Hosta* spp.)
PLANT CYCLE: Perennial, Zones 3–8
PREFERENCES: Plant in dappled to deep shade.
Hosta foliage is not truly silver in tone, but its variegated nature and ribbed texture are wonderful in the moon garden at night and lush and attractive in the daytime. Width and height depend on the particular species and variety. The leaves of *H*. 'Patriot' have bold, vivid white borders, making it excellent for moon gardens. Another excellent choice for the moon garden is *H. plantaginea*, which features fragrant white flowers in late summer.

Lamb's Ears (*Stachys byzantina*)
PLANT CYCLE: Perennial, Zones 4–9
PREFERENCES: Plant in full sun to partial shade; prefers rich, well-drained soil, but will tolerate dry conditions.
Lamb's ears makes a wonderful edging or border plant; it also does well in containers. It grows 8 to 12 inches tall and spreads yearly as a ground cover. Its flower spikes are insignificant compared to its soft, wooly, grayish-white foliage, which begs to be stroked. Plant lamb's ears in a spot where it can easily be touched.

Lavender (*Lavandula* spp.)
PLANT CYCLE: Perennial, Zones 5–8
PREFERENCES: Plant in full sun in dry, sandy soil.
Lavender's gray-green foliage, delicate fragrance, and neat spikes of lavender-blue blossoms make it a natural for the moon garden. For colder climates, English lavender (*L. angustifolia*) is quite hardy; when heavily mulched and planted in well-drained soil, it can survive a pretty harsh winter. Lavender will remain in bloom from summer to fall.

Russian Sage (*Perovskia atriplicifolia*)
PLANT CYCLE: Perennial, Zones 3–9
PREFERENCES: Plant in full sun in well-drained soil.
Also known as azure sage, this shrubby perennial practically glows at dusk. Its purple-blue flowers are tiny but numerous in mid- to late summer, and its stems and leaves are a delicate silver-white. Cutting the plants back to the ground in spring will improve blooming.

Plants with Light-Colored Flowers

Plants with white, near-white, or pastel flowers are welcome enough in the daytime, but they're truly memorable in the dusk and moonlit hours. Their luminous glow creates a sense of quiet and calm in the garden, encouraging visitors to spend time peaceably puttering about, chatting with each other or simply enjoying some time to themselves.

Astilbe (*Astilbe* spp.)
PLANT CYCLE: Perennial, Zones 4–8
PREFERENCES: Plant in partial to full shade in moist, well-drained soil.
A beautiful perennial for the moon garden, astilbe blooms from late spring through summer, depending on the species and variety. Astilbes often reach heights of 3 feet and spread to 16 inches across. Though individual astilbe blossoms are small, each branch bears hundreds of them, which rise in soft, feathery plumes above the fern-like foliage. There are numerous species and varieties with white or pastel flowers to choose from. Check with your local gardening center for suggestions of astilbes that do well in your region.

Baby's Breath (*Gypsophila elegans* and *G. paniculata*)
PLANT CYCLE: Perennial or annual, depending on the species
PREFERENCES: Grow in full sun in average, well-drained soil.
The species and variety determine the growth habit of this airy-textured plant, which features a virtual haze of tiny white flowers. *G. elegans* is an annual that reaches 18 to 24 inches in height and 12 inches in width. Varieties of *G. paniculata* are shrublike perennials hardy from Zones 4 to 8. 'Bristol Fairy', its best-known cultivar, has pure white double flowers and grows 3 feet high. Because its flowers are short-lived, sow baby's breath every two weeks to ensure continuous blooming throughout the growing season.

Balloon Flower (*Platycodon grandiflorus*)
PLANT CYCLE: Perennial, Zones 3–9
PREFERENCES: Plant in full sun to partial shade in rich, moist, well-drained soil.
This long-lived perennial is so named because its buds are completely round, resembling tiny balloons, before they open into wide-mouthed, upturned bells. Balloon flower blooms over a long period in the summer, forming a clump 18 to 24 inches high and wide. Flowers range in color from white to purple to blue.

Blazing Star *(Liatris spicata)*
PLANT CYCLE: Perennial, Zones 3–10
PREFERENCES: Plant in full sun; prefers fertile, sandy soil, but will tolerate most soil conditions.
Also known as gayfather, this strong perennial sends forth striking 3-foot flower spikes that are bewitching in a moon garden. Blazing star blooms from summer to early fall. For pure white flowers choose the varieties 'Alba' or 'Floristan White'.

Bleeding Heart *(Dicentra spectabilis)*
PLANT CYCLE: Perennial, Zones 3–9
PREFERENCES: Plant in partial shade in rich, moist, well-drained soil.
This elegant perennial is one of the most profusely flowering plants suitable for shady places. Bleeding heart has lovely fernlike foliage and sprays of heart-shaped pink and white blooms at the tips of long, slender stems reaching 2 to 3 feet in height.

Butterfly Bush *(Buddleia davadii)*
PLANT CYCLE: Perennial, Zones 5–9
PREFERENCES: Plant in full sun in well-drained soil; cut back nearly to the ground in spring for maximum bloom.
Butterfly bush is probably the most renowned butterfly-attracting plant; it will also attract a wide variety of beautiful night-flying moths. Butterfly bush grows 4 to 5 feet in height and width. Its flowers, which bloom from midsummer until the first frost, are richly scented and come in a range of colors. Two varieties that are especially nice in a moon garden are 'Harlequin', which has green foliage edged in white and rose-pink flowers, and 'White Profusion', which bears pure white blooms.

Butterfly bush

Calla Lily *(Zantedeschia aethiopica)*
PLANT CYCLE: Perennial, Zones 8–11
PREFERENCES: Plant in full sun in wet, fertile soil.
A perennial from South Africa, calla is grown as an annual in most of North America. Calla lily has bold, arrow-shaped leaves and elegant, funnel-shaped tropical white blossoms that rise 2 to 3 feet high. It performs well in a container. The variety 'Crowborough', with dark greenish red leaves and large white flowers, is particularly striking.

Candytuft *(Iberis amaru)*
PLANT CYCLE: Annual
PREFERENCES: Plant in full sun in average, well-drained soil.
This fragrant, old-fashioned annual performs beautifully in beds or containers. It grows

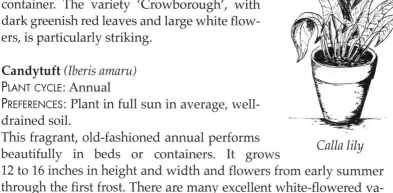

Calla lily

12 to 16 inches in height and width and flowers from early summer through the first frost. There are many excellent white-flowered varieties, including 'Iceberg', 'Mount Hood', and 'Pinnacle'.

Clematis *(Clematis cvs.)*
PLANT CYCLE: Perennial, Zones 4–9
PREFERENCES: Plant in full sun, underplanted with short annuals or with its roots protected by mulch.
A climbing perennial that reaches 6 to 8 feet high and 2 feet wide, clematis is marvelous for adorning a trellis, arbor, or fence. Most commonly grown clematis have eye-catching large, flat flowerheads; other species feature smaller blooms in varying shapes and sizes. Flowers are pink, purple, white, yellow, or cream.

Cleome *(Cleome hassleriana)*
PLANT CYCLE: Annual
PREFERENCES: Plant in full sun in light, sandy soil. Cleome will often reseed itself, if permitted.
Cleome is prized for their vivid flower spikes, which reach 5 feet in height. Long stamens give this plant an airy, graceful look — hence its common name, spider flower. 'Helen Campbell' is a popular white-flowering variety.

Clustered Bellflower *(Campanula glomerata)*
PLANT CYCLE: Perennial, Zones 3–8
PREFERENCES: Plant in full sun or partial shade in moist, well-drained soil.
Clustered bellflower features long flowers shaped like — what else? — bells. Flowers range in color from violet to lavender-blue to white and are borne all summer long. The plant reaches 18 inches in height and width. Clustered bellflowers are long-lived and rarely bothered by pests or disease. A good variety for the moon garden is 'Schneekrone' (syn. 'Crown of Snow'), which bears dense clusters of large white flowers. Other campanulas you might consider are *C. carpatica* 'Bresshingham White' and 'Weisse Clips', low-growing varieties with abundant white flowers; *C. cashmeriana* 'Superba', with striking lilac flowers; and *C. medium* 'Bells of Holland', a dwarf variety with abundant flowers in various pastel shades.

Coneflower *(Echinacea purpurea)*
PLANT CYCLE: Perennial, Zones 3–9
PREFERENCES: Plant in full sun in rich, well-drained soil.
An easy-to-grow perennial that is rarely bothered by pests or disease, coneflower reaches nearly 3 feet in height. It has sturdy stems, blooms for a long time in summer, and grows 12 to 14 inches wide. Good coneflower varieties for the moon garden are the white-flowering 'Finale White', 'White Lustre', and 'White Swan'.

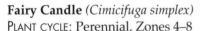
Coneflower

Fairy Candle *(Cimicifuga simplex)*
PLANT CYCLE: Perennial, Zones 4–8
PREFERENCES: Grow in moist, rich soil in partial shade.
What could be more fun than inviting fairies to your moon garden? Fairy candle — also known as black cohosh and snakeroot — grows 3 to 8 feet high and has wiry, branched stems. It features feathery racemes filled with tiny white blooms loftily displayed above the foliage, appearing suspended in the moonlight.

Dianthus (*Dianthus* cvs.)
PLANT CYCLE: Perennial, Zones 3–9, depending on the variety
PREFERENCES: Plant in full sun to partial shade.
These perennials are commonly known as "pinks" — not for their color, but for their ragged petals, which look like they've been cut with pinking shears. They grow 6 to 18 inches tall and spread into a tufted mound. Because of its compact growing shape, dianthus performs well in containers or as a border plant. There are many varieties that would complement a moon garden. Check in with your local gardening center for recommendations on white-flowering dianthus that do well in your area.

Flowering Tobacco (*Nicotiana sylvestris*)
PLANT CYCLE: Annual or short-lived perennial
PREFERENCES: Grow in full sun to partial shade in fertile, moist, well-drained soil.
A graceful, sun-loving plant, flowering tobacco reaches up to 4 feet in height. Although its trumpet-shaped blossoms are lovely, it is especially welcome in the moon garden because of its intoxicating fragrance. Dwarf varieties are also available; these are just as fragrant and grow well in containers.

Foxglove (*Digitalis purpurea*)
PLANT CYCLE: Biennial or short-lived perennial, Zones 4–8
PREFERENCES: Plant in partial shade; prefers rich soil but will tolerate most soil conditions.
This elegant and graceful self-seeding plant reaches 3 to 4 feet in height, spreading 24 inches. Foxglove presents its trumpet-shaped blooms on tall spikes that rise above the foliage. Search out those varieties that have white blossoms. *Caution:* Keep pets and children away from this plant, as it can be toxic if ingested.

Garden Phlox (*Phlox paniculata*)
PLANT CYCLE: Perennial, Zones 4–8
PREFERENCES: Plant in full sun or partial shade in fertile, moist soil.
Garden phlox is an old-time favorite among gardeners. This fragrant perennial reaches nearly 4 feet in height and spreads 16 inches. It blooms most of the summer on sturdy stems. The varieties 'David', 'Fujiyama', 'Mia Ruys', and 'White Admiral' have white blossoms. An especially beautiful variety is 'Franz Shubert', which features pale lilac-pink blooms.

Geranium (*Pelargonium* spp.)
PLANT CYCLE: Perennial, Zones 10–11
PREFERENCES: Growing preferences vary among species.
Given the proliferation of geranium species and cultivars, and their dependable blooming nature, it's no surprise that this trusty little plant can be found in many moon gardens. Most varieties are easy to grow, and many are also pleasantly scented. Geranium's low growth habit makes it perfect for containers or as a border plant. Search out those varieties that have white or pastel blooms.

Madagascar Periwinkle (*Catharanthus roseus*)
PLANT CYCLE: Tender perennial or annual
PREFERENCES: Grow in full sun or partial shade in fertile, well-drained soil.
This long-blooming tender perennial is perfect for beds, borders, containers, or hanging baskets. Madagascar periwinkle tolerates adverse growing conditions such as heat and drought and still blooms luxuriously. The Pacifica Series has pale pink to white blooms and reaches 10 to 12 inches in height; a particularly beautiful variety is 'Parasol', which has large white flowers marked with a dark pink eye. *Caution:* Keep pets and children away from this plant, as it can be toxic if ingested.

Obedient Plant (*Physostegia virginiana*)
PLANT CYCLE: Perennial, Zones 4–8
PREFERENCES: Plant in full sun or partial shade in fertile, moist soil.
Graceful stems covered with stunning vertical arrays of tubular pink, purple, or white flowers dominate this long-blooming perennial. It reaches 24 to 36 inches high and spreads 18 to 24 inches wide. White-flowered varieties include 'Alba', 'Crown of Snow', and 'Summer Snow'.

Petunia (*Petunia* cvs.)
PLANT CYCLE: Annual
PREFERENCES: Grow in well-drained soil in full sun.
One of the most beloved annuals, the petunia provides undiminished color through the season and is renowned for its versatility. Whatever the requirement, there is a petunia cultivar to fill the need. Some varieties are recommended for containers, since they cascade attractively over the edges. Others, such as the Floribundas, do well in mass plantings or in borders. The Carpet Series make a wonderful

ground cover as well as a container plant. White and pastel shades are available in each type. Deadhead for extended blooming.

Petunias

Plume Poppy *(Macleaya cordata)*
PLANT CYCLE: Perennial, Zones 4–9
PREFERENCES: Prefers full sun and fertile, moist, well-drained soil, but will tolerate most soils and some shade.
Perfect in the moon garden, plume poppy has large grayish leaves that are white and downy underneath, and its airy cream-colored blooms wave gracefully on strong stems. Plume poppy grows up to 8 feet tall, usually without needing to be staked, making it excellent as a specimen plant or to define the garden edges. The roots spread outward, so it can be somewhat invasive.

Rose *(Rosa* spp.)
PLANT CYCLE: Perennial
PREFERENCES: Most roses prefer full sun and fertile, moist, well-drained soil.
Nothing is quite so spectacular as the sight of white roses gleaming in the moonlight — except perhaps the delicate fragrance of roses sifting through the warm evening air. You can establish a rose bed as the centerpiece to your garden or use roses as accents, growing them on trellises and arbors on your garden paths. Miniature roses perform beautifully in borders or containers. There are many different varieties of white-blooming roses; check in with your local gardening center for suggestions.

Shasta Daisy *(Leucanthemum x superbum)*
PLANT CYCLE: Perennial, Zones 4–8
PREFERENCES: Plant in full sun in moist, well-drained soil.
Shasta daisy reaches from 12 to 36 inches high and spreads into a neat, mounded shape. It bears single or double white flowers, depending on the variety; all are easy to grow and dependable bloomers. Some popular white-flowering varieties include 'Alaska', 'Horace Read', and 'Polaris'.

Sneezewort *(Achillea ptarmica)*
PLANT CYCLE: Perennial, Zones 3–8
PREFERENCES: Plant in full sun in moist, well-drained soil.
Sneezewort is related to yarrow but looks more like a grandiose version of baby's breath. Trouble free and easy to grow, this plant produces an abundance of double, pure white blooms all summer long. It is a vigorous, sometimes floppy plant, but a compact variety called 'The Pearl', which reaches only 2 feet in height and less in width, is a big improvement over the species.

Spike Speedwell *(Veronica spicata)*
PLANT CYCLE: Perennial, Zones 3–8
PREFERENCES: Plant in full sun in fertile, moist, well-drained soil.
Speedwell blooms merrily most of the summer, reaching 16 inches high and 12 inches wide, with blooms displayed on elegant spikes that rise above the foliage. Speedwell comes in a range of colors; white-blooming varieties include 'Alba', 'Icicle', and 'Noah Williams'. The silvery gray foliage of *V. spicata* subsp. *incana* is also interesting in a moon garden.

Spike speedwell

Stock *(Matthiola incana)*
PLANT CYCLE: Perennial, biennial, or annual, depending on the variety
PREFERENCES: Grow in full sun in a moist, well-drained soil.
This wonderful old-fashioned garden flower reaches 18 to 30 inches in height, depending on the variety. Stock

can be grown in containers and is excellent as a border planting because of its precise growth habits. It is exceptionally fragrant and provides color for the entire growing season. White flowers abound in each of the different cultivar groups; ask your local gardening center for suggestions.

Sweet Alyssum *(Lobularia maritima)*
PLANT CYCLE: Annual
PREFERENCES: Plant in full sun in light, average soil.
Sweet alyssum is wonderful as a border or edging plant or even in containers and hanging baskets. It grows only 6 inches high and spreads to 8 inches wide, and its profuse blooms have a delightful fragrance. 'Carpet of Snow' and 'Snow Crystals' are two common white-flowered varieties.

Tuberose *(Polianthes tuberosa)*
PLANT CYCLE: Tender perennial
PREFERENCES: Grow in full sun in well-drained soil.
A tender perennial grown from a tuber that can be dug in the fall and replanted the following spring, tuberose has extraordinary fragrant white blooms. This versatile plant is perfect for growing in containers and spectacular when massed in beds or borders. The variety 'The Pearl' has semi-double porcelain white blossoms.

Night-Blooming Plants

The true stars of the moon garden are, of course, those rare plants that bloom only at night. These delicate wonders are often intoxicatingly fragrant and always dazzlingly beautiful.

Angel's Trumpet *(Brugmansia* spp. and *Datura* spp.)
PLANT CYCLE: Perennial, Zones 9–10
PREFERENCES: Grow in full sun in rich, moist soil.
This native of the tropics is usually grown as an annual in North America. A vigorous grower, it reaches 5 to 6 feet in height in just a few weeks and prefers full sun. True to its name, angel's trumpet bears exquisite, large, trumpet-shaped white flowers. The flowers don't close during the day, but they come to life at night, when they release their luxurious fragrance. *Caution:* Keep pets and children away from this plant, as it is highly toxic if ingested.

Daylily (*Hemerocallis* spp.)
PLANT CYCLE: Perennial, Zones 3–10, depending on the species
PREFERENCES: Grow in full sun in fertile, moist, well-drained soil.
Daylily may not sound like a promising name for a night-blooming plant, but, in fact, there are many species of daylilies that bloom in the evening, stay open all night, and then close in the morning. Other daylilies' blooms stay open for 16 hours or more, from the early morning well into the late evening. Check in with your local gardening center for recommendations on night-blooming or extended-blooming daylilies that do well in your region.

Evening Primrose (*Oenothera* spp.)
PLANT CYCLE: Perennial or biennial, Zones 4–8, depending on the species
PREFERENCES: Grow in full sun in fertile, well-drained soil.
Evening primrose comes in countless sizes and colors, depending on the species, many of which are prized for their nocturnal flowers. If you have the patience, sit by the plant at dusk, watching carefully. Slowly but irrepressibly, the blossoms open before your eyes. Interesting species for the moon garden include *O. macrocarpa,* the Missouri primrose, with large, light yellow flowers; *O. acaulis,* with white flowers that fade to pink; *O. argillicola,* with bright yellow flowers; *O. californica,* with white flowers that fade to pink; and *O. erythrosepal,* which has small, bright yellow flowers.

Moonflower *(Ipomoea alba)*
PLANT CYCLE: Tender perennial or annual
PREFERENCES: Plant in full sun in average, well-drained soil.
A relative of the common morning glory, this tender perennial twining vine is practically synonymous with moon gardens. Its showy white blossoms open in the evening to dazzle the beholder all night. Grow moonflower on a trellis, let it spill from baskets or boxes, or twine it around porch posts. Moonflower's seed coat is hard, which makes it slow to germinate. Nick the seeds with

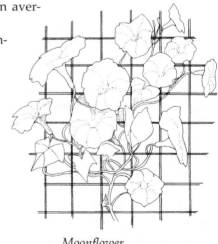

Moonflower

a knife, and then soak them overnight in warm water before planting to speed up germination. 'Giant White' bears huge white flowers up to 6 inches across.

Tropical Water Lilies (*Nymphaea* spp.)
PLANT CYCLE: Perennial, Zones 10–11
PREFERENCES: Plant in full sun to partial shade with 6 to 18 inches of water over the crowns, depending on the variety.
With their striking flowers, water lilies add a touch of the exotic to the moon garden. There are many night-blooming varieties available. Check in with your local gardening center for recommendations on night-blooming water lilies that do well in your area.

Container Moon Gardens

If your garden space is limited, you can create a delightful moon garden on your deck or patio by using container plants. Careful arranging and grouping of the containers can produce a striking effect. If the containers are large enough, you can even combine several plants.

Many plants that are suitable for a moon garden bed grow equally well in containers. And some, such as tuberose, perfume your entire patio with a heavenly fragrance.

Select Suitable Containers

The containers you use can be as plain or as elaborate as you wish. Clay, plastic, and ceramic pots; wooden or plastic window boxes; and plastic and wire baskets lined with sphagnum moss are commonly used. But don't limit yourself to these choices; let your imagination roam. For example, window boxes are versatile planters that are not just for windows. Hang them from porch railings or walls, or use them to mark the edges of a deck or patio, to line walkways, or to define the edges of your garden.

> ### Quick Container Tip
>
> If you want to use a container that does *not* have drainage holes, such as a pail or a ceramic bowl, first place the plant in a pot that *can* drain. Then display the pot inside the pail or bowl, using a layer of stones to keep the pot above the water level so the roots aren't constantly wet. You can employ the same method with containers that can't hold soil, such as loosely woven baskets.

How to Prepare a Container

For containers with drainage holes, first line the inside of the container with a piece of fine mesh screen. This prevents the soil from leaking out and creating a mess on the patio while still permitting drainage. On top of the mesh, add a layer of small rocks or pebbles, then good-quality potting soil. Fill the pot with soil to the same level at which the plant is growing, and then add the plant. Firm the soil around the rootball, but don't press *too* firmly; if you do, you will eliminate air and make the soil too compact. Water well. Feed container-growing plants weekly with a water-soluble plant food.

Good Container Plants

Consider some or all of the following for your container moon garden:

- Sweet alyssum
- Angel's trumpet
- Calla lily
- Candytuft
- Dianthus
- Dusty miller
- Flowering tobacco
- Geranium
- Impatiens
- Petunia
- Tuberose

Hanging and Climbing Gardens

If space is a problem, think vertical instead of horizontal. Hang cascading baskets of white and pastel flowers everywhere. Group them at different levels for visual appeal, or hang them from nearby tree limbs. Create a floral pillar by suspending them from a rack designed for that purpose. Hanging baskets can also adorn walls and fences.

Stack pots of tuberose, impatiens, and geraniums into tiered groupings around a chair or bench, forming a cozy haven where you can relax. You can also create a snug little nook by using trellises attached to planters. Some wonderful climbing plants are:

- Clematis
- Moonflower
- Climbing roses
- White morning glory